Mourning
is
Women's Business

Mourning
is
Women's Business

Lee Cataldi

PUNCHER & WATTMANN

First published in 2023
Published by Puncher and Wattmann
PO Box 279
Waratah NSW 2298

https://www.puncherandwattmann.com
web@puncherandwattmann.com

ISBN   9781922571359

Cover design by David Musgrave
Typesetting by Morgan Arnett
Printed by Lightning Source International

A catalogue record for this
work is available from the
National Library of Australia

Contents

c'est l'homme   7

Balgo Poems

Aaron   11

history: black arm band   12

mangoes   13

mourning is women's business   14

reservayion blues   17

road kills   18

tears   19

the opening of the children's centre in Balgo   20

In the Empire of Breathing

Luggage

visit   23

hereafter   24

Itinerary

Jaisalmer   25

in the course of a day   26

coloured slides   27

India's daughters   29

the Gurgaon road   30

Dussehra   31

Delhi's winter   32

India's boys   33

Bombay goes to work   34

TV in Trivandrum   35

being ill in India   36

the college students   37

on the passing of ted hughes: a warning   38

Mahabalipuram   39

Indra's kitchen   40

playing sport in India   41

Finale

todi   43

mandolin   45

midnight at Madras airport   46

Here it will burn

Israel   49

sherpa   50

the sky is falling in   51

on breaking things   52

broken hearts   53

the field stands silent   54

seventy   55

carol 2019   56

Translations

michelangelo   59

michelangelo   60

michelangelo   61

mallarmé   62

mallarmé   64

mallarmé   65

c'est l'homme

for John Forbes

                          you
develope a style until
it can say what you want   you need   it may
take years and years

of need   a style
is a bit like a life
                          and then
it comes together
style   book   life
                          and then
much to your surprise
this neat construction
falls apart

there is no book
the life is not what was planned
and the style
seems hopelessly out of date and
immortality a fading dream but

the need
turns out to be timeless

and in the house there is
some small drug or other
to tide you over
                          and the style
takes a mini cooper and throws it
down like a gauntlet

and choosing a word is again
the first mouthful of something
brilliant and daring
always perfect

          and you know
despite all the stumbling about in the bushes
the stubbed toes   the dirt   the broken fingernails

there was a kind of twisted little track
leading to the photo opportunity at the top of the cliff
and from there you can see

a mini cooper burning in the snow

perfect

Balgo Poems

Aaron

Aaron Baajo Japangardi age
fourteen of Balgo   doesn't want
his aunt's stories or her dreams
of an outstation at a spot
where two men changed the universe

                              he wants
to fuck and take drugs and get
his gorgeous arse to dance parties

                         and be picked up
by rich older men

history: black arm band

they are crying for a girl
lost in the darkness   drunk
on a lonely road
                          taken they say
there by a white man

and cut in two
by at least one vehicle

their musical lament
with infinite sadness
is for all the ngantany
lost since the first one
was taken by a white man

somewhere to a lonely place

and cut in two

mangoes

suddenly I saw us
eating mangoes   all
inhibitions gone   drunk again
and young

          our faces
pressed against each other   our noses
deep in sweet yellow mango flesh

          our eyes
blinded with pink mango light

surrounded by crushed and rotting fruit together
under the hot dark tree

mourning is women's business

for Tjama

1

with a gesture as large as the planet
you call up the spirits of women
tonight you can see them   thousands
filling up the country so it is
no longer empty

and lonely as it will be
when you are gone

and the multitudes no longer
dance across the spinifex

2

you were dancing
a slow skip
in the grand style
wearing a striped pointed hat
and white ochre
all your golden hair
cut to the grey

you go on without them like those
wounded in the leg
limping

dancing towards the embrace of the others
who limping
dance towards you

when the circles of recognition are complete
after days and weeks of sitting in the dust
you can get up wash go home
back to your places of employment

and the free spirit will burst
out of this belly of grief
into the air

3

when you were young you went to law
childless but free

now the funerals string together
narratives of loss
                              how hard it is
to think any more of forever

sometimes
you want private you want
out fold your shirt over your chest
and yourself up to sleep
your stomach hurts
with grief

when you were young and went about your business
who would have thought it would end
covered in white clay in a row of widows
seeing the land losing its people

your stomach hurts
and it's hard to breathe

reservation blues

one road leads to the airstrip
and one road leads to town
and I would take either of these
if I could put the money down

the children are wild like dogs
and the dogs as hungry as the kids
you don't have to be Saint Peter to see
the place is on the skids

it's fourteen kilometers from Malan
and forty kilometers from home
where the boys go on cutting the wire
and no-one is ever alone

my grannies lived in the bush
before the white man came
they talk about the spirits
but for me it's just not the same

road kills

the road a black strip
an opportune vein
across it are flung
the bodies of natives some
so fresh their fur
fans in the wind

their nailed hands out
as if asking a question
or folded across their chests
as if praying
for an answer

tears

your tears
are warm upon my face
would be
warmer on my thigh
your tears

              undoing
history could stop them

my history

the opening of the children's centre in Balgo

a smell of frying meat
drifts across the scene
and steam
from bloodwood leaves assists
departing souls to leave

a tiny child
hurls a rock across the yard
some skills die hard

it is as if the language
centre that was here
had never been   the kukatja books
into which we put
our black and white lives have become
art works no-one can read

these days Balgo is a picture

and for sale

In the Empire of Breathing

Luggage

visit

even if they arrive
incarnate apparently   smeared
white with clay or ash
or caked with black dust with such
warmth of welcome such
smiles of pure delight

we are so pleased to see them but
waking in the real dawn our
mouths parch with horror
                                        these
friendly and beautiful dead

inhabit us

hereafter

you should have died much later

                                there would have been

a space for such an event

                                you could have been

properly translated to a star
magical mysterious a new
inhabitant of heaven

not in such complete silence we
did not even know you had gone

all that remains is an absence
and a gravestone in another country

like slides in a lantern that lost summer
revives but scratched   faded   with pieces missing

like so much else
the sky above us   the ground
under our feet
damaged imperfect but
all we have

Itinerary

Jaisalmer

opium your mother   silver
your father a
paradise in sand golden
as that which surrounds you once
oasis of such pleasures   now
the dancers have fallen
on hard times   those who played
on balconies suspended in the stars
are singing for tourists
down in the street

merchants who sold
brocade to crowned heads
search for such visitors as will understand
this miraculous
conservative
decadent city
not being taken in

by the alien customs
of those who have just arrived

in the course of a day

Jaipur wakes to the smell of burning
rubbish when the wind
blows from where the bus from Delhi
gets its first view of the city

but in the evening breeze
the smoke reminds me impossibly
of barbecues   blowing
from funerals in Bani Park

coloured slides

hotel Uphar, Shimla

vertical city astonishingly steep
perched at the pinnacle this hotel

Viceregal Lodge

passionate speech now
a terrible careless decision taken
in this same room

Sanskriti Kendra

the humidity increases
sudden almost silent rain falls

travelling

here I am as lonely
as a mosque in Rajasthan

this just about sums it up

as the bus
pitched off the shoulder of the road
roll with the punches
was the last thing
she thought about India

passing train passengers

dishevelled but awake
a book and a white foreign leg
perch by a window

wet

a monsoon climate
commits
murder on paper

India's daughters

faces of luminous sweetness
in tight jeans and brothel creepers
with windcheaters
named after immigrant cities

at a distance
marriage seems as lovely
as Shimla at night but
up close in daylight
a rust eaten mountain

India's daughters
when the inevitable happens
take up their burdens
as porters
                        try to balance
impossible weight

and impossible climb

the Gurgaon road

the road   victim
of many trucks   trucks victim
of endless collages   major
and minor repairs   the road

not the garden is
where it all happens   thrift
and desperation   also
its laneways
                    opening into
wasp nests of commerce

milled
between scooters and buses are whole
enterprises
                    dwellings   markets

by day
it is a torrent   at night
its groaning elderly engines
wind past reminding us

of what is done
to survive

Dussehra

ANZ Bank Connaught Place
Delhi 1998

in the clean
draft of air filtered
cooled a man very slowly
writes figures in a large notebook

while girls with computers whizz
through the real transactions   the bank
looks like ours at home but no-one
has enquiry on their desk
or answers questions

it's a showpiece
a bank theatre in a land
whose government is Ram Lila played
on a giant chariot with huge wheels dragged
by the millions who choke
in Ravana's evil-smelling white smoke
their stomachs growling with Ravana's dog hunger their feet
tramping his littered kingdom   their last breath
escaping under the weight
of his hand

Delhi's winter

was delicate
still light mist
feathery leaves

now
an umbrella that traps
poisonous gas
day after day

India's boys

climb over train seats and tread on
their sisters   unreproved jump
on whatever they find in their way
boys will be boys even when
limping old men

congregate like flies
around strip joints and bars
whatever country
they find themselves in
but virtuous and vegetarian
at home

                        in clothes
immaculately pressed
by wives and mothers
undisputed rulers
of public spaces

a girl on the street navigates
enemy territory
a girl on a train
is a hostage
her fate is uncertain

the boys will decide
if she gets home

Bombay goes to work

and comes home again   hanging
out of doorways and windows
on the train
                        when it stops
dreadful smells rise up from the tracks
a girl prays   her lips
move rapidly across pages handed
down the ages   I squash
a centipede with my shoe
and take the blame   two

women in saris plant
their legs between mine   we
sway in unison and across
the sea of heads floats
green as health and sweet
as morning the scent

of ripe guavas

TV in Trivandrum

lying on the bed watching
BBC world programmed
for executives drifting in space

insulates me
from the dust falling into this room
from the dark crowded street
full of ditches and vehicles
from the bright crippled boy
begging outside the airport who said in English
I'm handicapped   and managed
from the ground to help me with my bags
I can see that   I said
and gave him 20 rupees
                              the TV
encapsulates all this waste
in silver globules of talk
                         for example
100 million starving Indonesians   until

disaster crashes through the picture
and the power goes off

being ill in India

gives you
a whole new view of it   as if
the great crescendo
of filth and disease
is homing in on you

suddenly you have to notice
what you can no longer try to ignore
the poor

weak with hunger and sick as you are
with infection
it is they who fetch and carry
clean and mend
as you lie in your hotel room hoping somehow

all this will end

the college students

their feet
glittering with the different ornaments
of the street

arrive in groups always
at least
fifteen minutes late but they

arrive like bunches of flowers
scattering into seats
                        their heads
sometimes with flowers
in their thick glossy black plaits

nodding
                     a breeze
limpid and fresh
that enters the room
each time they do

on the passing of ted hughes: a warning

when I go
there must be left no
statements of belief nothing
about the dictatorship of the proletariat the
labor theory of value

empty the cupboards like the mind
before the event
or like an Indian institution put
the centuries of old files to rot
in an outhouse on the roof

Mahabalipuram

for C.T. Indra

the sea is alive with gods
it blows them in mouthfuls
up on the beach

                    they
take up residence
amongst the rocks

the rocks are now
alive with gods
waking and sleeping

singing and laughing   their arms stretched
companionably over the shoulders
even of humans

Indra's kitchen

the spat
of mustard seeds in oil   the hiss
from the pressure cooker
the god beside the door

Arjuna
the act must be devoid of self
its outcome is itself

potatoes   green chili   curry leaves
gourd   four foods

Arjuna
it is the act which is offered to the god
to the mighty wings
beating beside the door

playing sport in India

for Meenakshi S

outside the small
apartment block in Jayanagar
Bangalore Adhitiya
swings his bat
                    from the TV on the floor
above he can hear the score

on Sunday in Chennai the boys
immaculate in white
dive and slide
across a filthy swamp   the pitch a line
in the mind's eye
and the MAC stadium
just a hit away

                high
above Beach Road a jet
crosses the sky
                looking up
from the slips a boy
sees himself gazing
down upon a sea of hands
all waving

                    sport
in India
is the subject of endless talk
somewhere to go between
sleep and work   more
dependable than eating   except
for the Rajput polo teams muttering
into the microphone er ah uh
                    as inarticulate
as the stars
of any other nation

playing sport in India is a dream
outside karma and dharma
outside the maya
where matches are fixed and bookies
have prior information
                    outside
the fight to stay alive

Finale

todi

if I could
unwind you slowly
from your sari   unfurl
the crispy tendrils of your hair
into the breeze   kiss
the tender whorls behind your ear
alone on a beach
                        between
the gods of the forest
the gods of the sea

we would offer ourselves thus
up to the elements
transfigured by joy   as when in song
the voice of the god
issues forth from the mouth
of your uncle the accountant

your tiny hands
your fawn translucent brahmin skin
daughter
of scholars and musicians   born
between rice field and water
small
bolt of lightning   child
of the luminous south

my people
if they will not
kill for love   will
die for it
for the lord of love yours
will try to live

the singer's voice
is a flame
that flickers on his face
the violin repeats
this play of light
and about them winds the beat
of hands on baked earth
of fingers on skin

this is my music
a fiery argument
concerning passion   your songs
do they transmute
all this burning
back into breathing

the violinist's forehead
runs with sweat   rain
drums on the roof introducing
the smell of wet leaves
the raga ends
we collect our shoes and move

out to the waiting taxi

mandolin

the boy
has electric tastes   I
am reminded
of Hendrix at Woodstock
playing to the sky

this boy
is a burner   he
isn't a breather
his sound zings
out to infinity
and comes back as a spark
its position is destiny but
its trajectory

is desire

midnight at Madras airport

where is he going   alone without
his family his friends   his sandals
restitched
by a pavement shoemaker
his small bag
carefully locked
his worn trousers and his face
patient as a quiet lesser god
lifting a beam or pulling a cart
the innocent hopeful face of working India

where is he going

to whatever god-forsaken hell
such labourers go

Here it will burn

Israel

I would arrest Israel
for insulting Jewishness
for offending
our semitic past
for terror and ethnic cleansing

for breaking the glass
of Palestinian shops and
Lebanese apartment blocks

for building walls   Stalag
Gaza and Stalag
West Bank

look in the mirror
at what you have become
dark hair white skin

little moustache

sherpa

when the mountain splits
the guides die   the guides
who are always there
always die

                    the client
whose presence demands a guide
goes over the edge
only by chance

the sky is falling in

I drive along in my car
destroying the planet
towing a horse
listening to the cricket

        the world
does not look as if it is about to end
but I know it will

       here
it will burn

on breaking things

a clumsy movement of the sleeve sweeps
the blown glass puja bell to the floor
and breaks the handle   one in a set

of such moves   hasty   uncontrolled   the snarl
the snap   the gesture
of impatience and irritation that breaks

more than the bell   the whole
enterprise   something which like the bell is delicate but signifies
much more than itself   a window

onto another universe
snapped off in effigy
before the music could begin

broken hearts

the horse
dropped dead in the straight in the last
race on what had been
a perfect afternoon from
the top of the members' stand the hay
fields reached the horizon the
breeze was cool despite the sun the track
was green

when they got
the blood sample to the lab it was
a perfect cocktail of nasties
                              before
the race they yelled to the jockey
a local star
                you got
to flog him   he's
a real loser

but the horse tried
he ran
so hard he died

the field stands silent

the vixen
has gone to ground

the horse
canters on into darkness

when the time comes
don't look at the mare

when the time comes
don't think of the bullet

when the time comes
lie down
surrounded by hounds

seventy

sometimes
you crap in the bath

      worry
about children with baseball bats
think of getting a gun
      just for the noise

even if you're prime minister you're in
the nuisance class
      everyone
thinks it unfair you have
anything at all

      my advice

give away as much as you can
it will
buy you time

carol 2019

smoke from the fires drifts overhead   what
will happen to our grandchildren

tiny figures playing in the dust
all over the planet   no
water in the river   no
rain ever   land
and belongings reduced to ash   what

does this tell us
about what we are doing?

Translations

michelangelo

27

you who kiss run   from
love's burning tongue   his
flames are savage his
cuts mortal he
fights to the death

after the first rush nothing
neither effort nor brains nor
leaving the country
will do any good   go

you see in me a staggering example
of the sharpness of his tooth
the strength of his arm his
bent disgusting game   when first

your eyes meet his
don't hang around   I thought
I could have him
any way I wanted   now

see what I am

michelangelo

107

my eyes   wild for beautiful things
and my mind have no other means
to get to heaven except
these blow them there

from the highest stars
a splendour descends
which draws desire in their direction
this is love

only this makes the true heart
burn   this and its mirror
a face in whose eyes
it can perceive the same

michelangelo

143

as pieces of my life fall away
each day smaller and fewer remaining
compressed
                    into this shrinking space the fire
burns more ferociously   and the sky
has never been known to lend a hand
to an old lag in a tight place   you know
even this is not enough   a passion
so hot stone might forget itself
let alone desire   I'm thankful
shut in these flames my heart
cannot last   and so I escape
life as your victim   you have no
interest in the dead

mallarmé

sea change

the body complains unfortunately and I've read all the books
shall I run away to where it is warmer? I believe birds
get drunk on the void between spray and sky

nothing   not the familiar gardens seen on gazing into eyes
will keep back those who plunge into the sea
on such nights   not the desert clarity of my lamp
on the blank paper's forbidding white
nor the young woman feeding her baby

no I'm going   the steamer with its jutting spar
sets off for a world of strangeness

boredom is made worse by such hopes
and always falls for the handkerchief waving goodbye
but maybe these masts cruising for storms
are the sort that a gale sucks into a wreck and
we are lost   dismasted   far from green islands
but desire listen

        to the song of the sailors

mallarmé

exhalations

towards your face calm sister where dreams
an autumn touched with russet towards
the wandering sky of your angel eye
I look up

                    from a dull garden
a faithful jet of white water
rises into the blue

this blue softened by pale October
which sees its own failure to act
reflected in ponds and on water
where the bright death of leaves
is a cold whistle in the wind which abandons

a last long yellow ray of sun

mallarmé

innocent breathless beautiful day

what does not fly
is not remembered
a sheet of ice
a hard lake
these you could free
with one drunk flap of your wing

the fabulous hopeless
out of date swan
can never escape
the shining places
the useless winter
his boredom inhabits

on the bird who denies it
space inflicts
a pain in the neck
which saves him of course
from sunburnt feathers

a transparent ghost the swan
has distilled himself
into this place and freezes
into a dream of being
misunderstood   his

exile is useless

www.ingramcontent.com/pod-product-compliance
Lightning Source LLC
Chambersburg PA
CBHW030813090426
42737CB00010B/1261